1878
Butterstamp

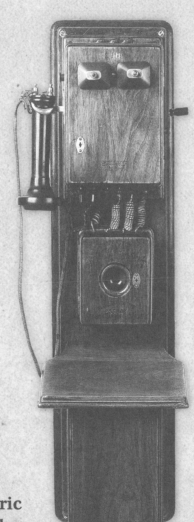

1882
Western Electric
Magneto Wall Phone

1896
Western Electric
Common Battery
Wall Phone

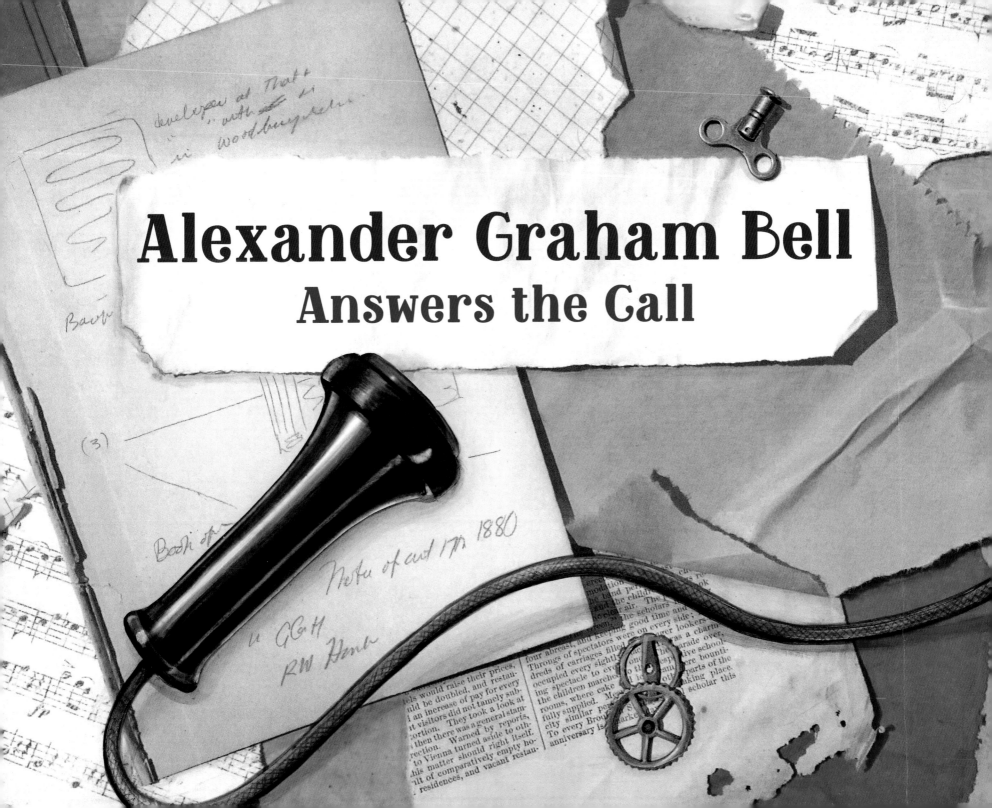

Alexander Graham Bell

Answers the Call

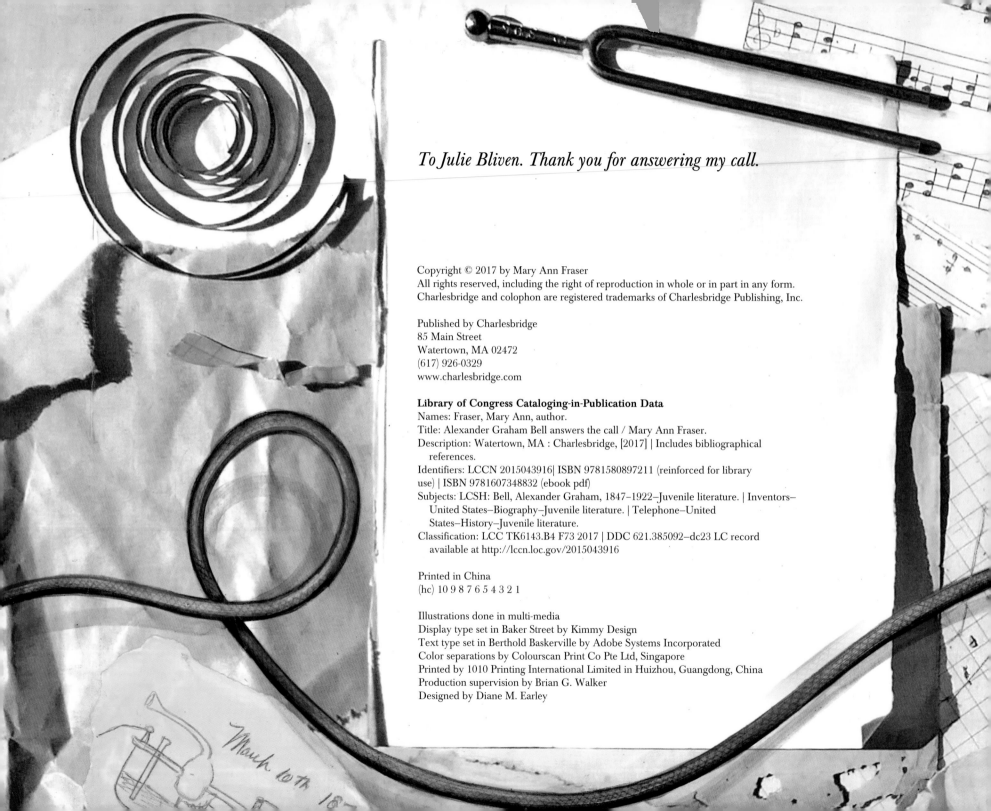

To Julie Bliven. Thank you for answering my call.

Published by Charlesbridge
85 Main Street
Watertown, MA 02472
(617) 926-0329
www.charlesbridge.com

Library of Congress Cataloging-in-Publication Data
Names: Fraser, Mary Ann, author.
Title: Alexander Graham Bell answers the call / Mary Ann Fraser.
Description: Watertown, MA : Charlesbridge, [2017] | Includes bibliographical
    references.
Identifiers: LCCN 2015043916| ISBN 9781580897211 (reinforced for library
use) | ISBN 9781607348832 (ebook pdf)
Subjects: LCSH: Bell, Alexander Graham, 1847–1922–Juvenile literature. | Inventors–
    United States–Biography–Juvenile literature. | Telephone–United
    States–History–Juvenile literature.
Classification: LCC TK6143.B4 F73 2017 | DDC 621.385092–dc23 LC record
    available at http://lccn.loc.gov/2015043916

Printed in China
(hc) 10 9 8 7 6 5 4 3 2 1

Illustrations done in multi-media
Display type set in Baker Street by Kimmy Design
Text type set in Berthold Baskerville by Adobe Systems Incorporated
Color separations by Colourscan Print Co Pte Ltd, Singapore
Printed by 1010 Printing International Limited in Huizhou, Guangdong, China
Production supervision by Brian G. Walker
Designed by Diane M. Earley

From the beginning, the world all around spoke to Alexander Graham Bell. And he listened. His family called him Aleck. To his eager ears, the hustle and bustle of 1840s Edinburgh, Scotland, was a symphony of every pitch and tone.

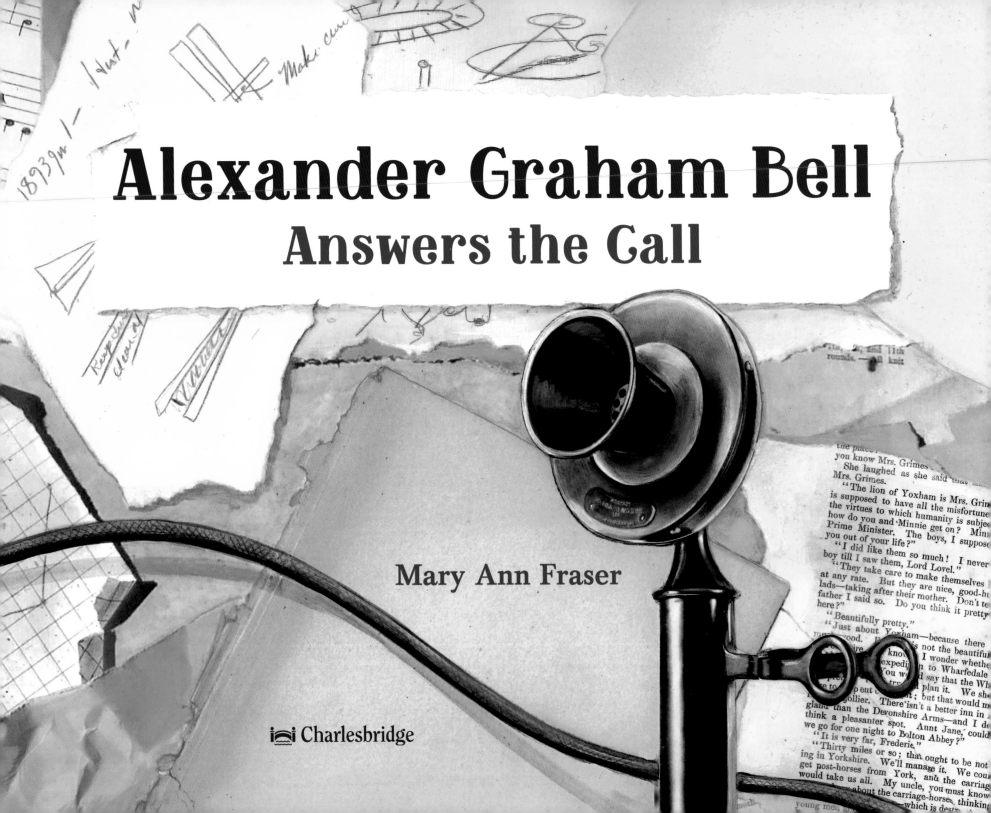

He even wandered into a field once to see if he could hear the wheat grow. Each new sound whispered to Aleck's curiosity. How was he able to hear? What made one noise different from another? Why could he hear some sounds but not others?

A-a-a-leck!
Where ar-r-e yo-u-u-u?

SWISH SWOOSH SWISH SWOOSH

A New Name

Aleck was born Alexander Melville Bell—the same name as his father and grandfather. But he adopted his cousin's middle name—Graham—because he liked how it sounded.

Aleck's father also had lots of questions about sound and hearing. Melville Bell was a speech therapist. The hisses, grunts, and chants of his students spilled from his study where he worked on his Visible Speech alphabet.

The symbols of this alphabet were different from the English language alphabet. They represented every sound made by the human voice. Aleck eagerly memorized all one hundred twenty-nine of them.

Visible Speech Flash Cards

B-B-B-B-B

While Aleck trained his ears to the sounds of speech, his mother heard little of it. Eliza Bell had lost most of her hearing as a child. Still, she was a gifted portrait painter and pianist, filling their home with art and song. To hear notes, she lay an ear tube across the piano's soundboard.

Aleck had to speak into the same ear tube for his mother to understand him. The awkward device acted like a hearing aid, but a poor one at best. How he wished he could find a better way for his mother to clearly hear his voice, the piano, the world around them.

Antibiotics to the Rescue

Before antibiotics became available in 1942, many children lost their hearing to infection and illness. In time, if they didn't get the proper help, they often forgot how to speak.

Along with his brothers, Melly and Ted, Aleck
learned to play the piano before he could read.
Sometimes the music rang in his mind for days.
He'd lay awake at night puzzling over how
instruments produced notes. How were he and
his brothers able to hear the notes when his
mother needed the aid of an ear tube?

His father explained that sounds are vibrations. Unlike his mother's, Aleck's ears were able to collect the vibrations and send the information to his brain. Of course Aleck had to test this notion out for himself. Could other parts of his body sense sound vibration, too?

TWAAAAANNNG

How the Ear Works

sound waves →

eardrum

to the brain

hair cells

cochlea

ear bones

1. The outer ear collects the sound waves.
2. Sound waves cause the eardrum to vibrate.
3. The ear bones transfer the vibrations to the cochlea.
4. Fluid in the cochlea stimulates the hair cells.
5. The hair cells inside the cochlea send electrical messages to the brain.

In his deepest voice, Aleck spoke close to his mother's forehead. By feeling his breath and the vibration of each sound against her skin, she could understand many of his words without the ear tube. His experiment had worked.

But at noisy gatherings, his mother still strained to make out what others were saying. There had to be a better way to include her. Aleck's answer was to use a two-handed manual alphabet to spell people's words with his fingers into his mother's palm. At last she could be part of the conversation.

Two-handed Communication

The two-handed manual alphabet was not as common as traditional sign language. But it allowed Aleck to signal letters on his mother's fingers, knuckles, and palm. For example, a touch to the ring finger is the sign for the letter "o."

While Aleck loved to study and experiment with sound, oh what fun he had showing off with it! When friends and relatives visited, he pounded the piano keys and belted out songs with Ted and Melly. Together they performed puppet shows and mimicked animals.

ZZ-ZZ-ZZ

Aleck's favorite voice trick was to race
about the room as if chasing a bee–*BUZZZ*.
He would then muffle his buzzing after pretending
to catch the insect in his hands.

For a boy with a head full of questions, it was an exciting time. It was the Age of Invention, and people everywhere were searching for new ways to solve old problems. Aleck was no different.

The Age of Invention

The steam engine of the late 1700s replaced human power with steam power. The rapid growth of factories changed the way people worked. A five-day trip by carriage soon turned into a one-day trip by train, and steamships cut transatlantic crossings from forty days to twelve. All these changes made the mid-1800s a time of great learning and innovation.

One day at a flour mill, Aleck wondered if he could find a better way to clean the grain. He lined the inside of an old churn with stiff brushes. With each crank, the churn's paddles pushed the grain against the brushes and whisked away the husks. Aleck listened to the sweeping noises of his first invention. What else could he invent?

CLANKETY-CLANK
CLANKETY-CLANK

A talking machine was the answer. Together he and his older brother, Melly, rigged up a rubber tongue, tin tube throat, and voice box. The downstairs neighbor thought the sound from the boys' contraption was a crying baby.

The Brothers' Talking Machine

1. Melly's breath blew through the tinplate tube at the back of the talking head, passing two sheets of rubber that acted like vocal cords.
2. His breath's vibration on the rubber created sound.
3. A resonance chamber similar to a nasal passage then amplified the sound.
4. At the same time, Aleck cranked a lever, moving the mouth parts, which changed the vibrations into humanlike speech sounds.

Aleck's noisy pranks didn't stop there. He trained the family's terrier to growl on command, and then moved its mouth and throat to produce different sounds. To everyone in the room it sounded as if the dog was saying, "How are you, Grandmama?"

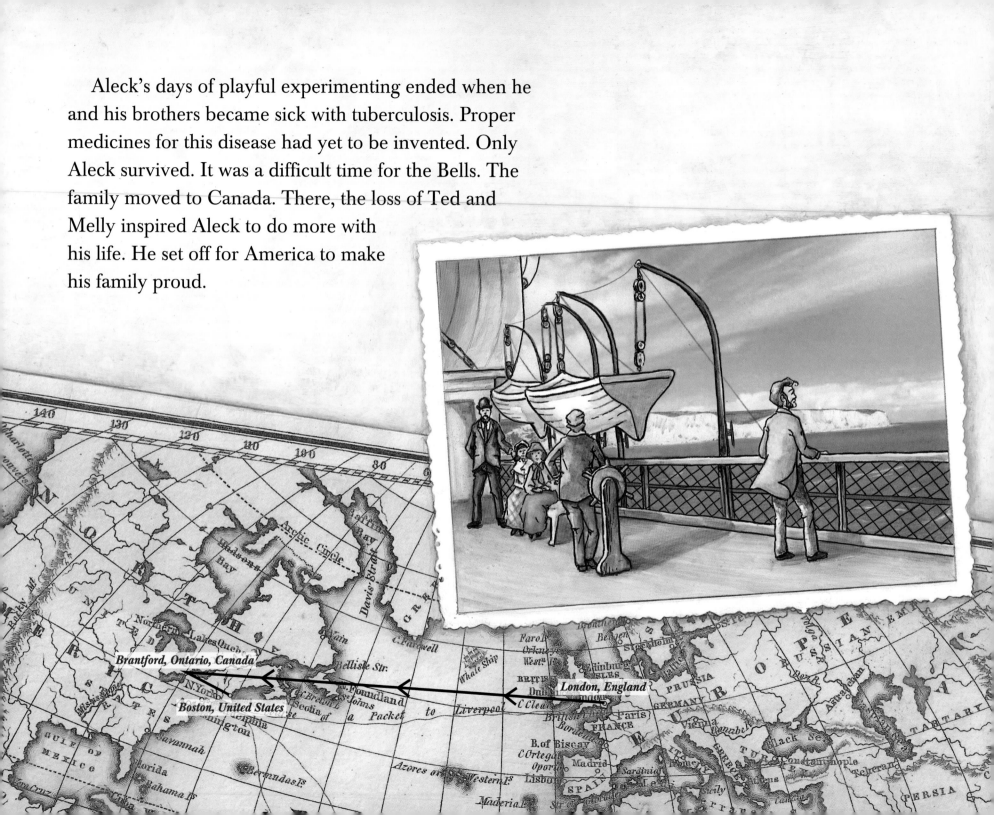

Aleck's days of playful experimenting ended when he and his brothers became sick with tuberculosis. Proper medicines for this disease had yet to be invented. Only Aleck survived. It was a difficult time for the Bells. The family moved to Canada. There, the loss of Ted and Melly inspired Aleck to do more with his life. He set off for America to make his family proud.

Brantford, Ontario, Canada

Boston, United States

London, England

Aleck's Alphabet Glove

In Boston, Massachusetts, Aleck became a teacher for the deaf. He taught his students sign language, lipreading, and Visual Speech. He also invented an alphabet glove. Students pointed to the letters printed on the glove to spell out messages. Each innovation whispered to Aleck's curiosity. What more could he do?

Aleck often wrote to his family about his lessons and ideas, but his letters took weeks, sometimes months to arrive. The telegraph was faster, but it was expensive and sent only one message in code at a time.

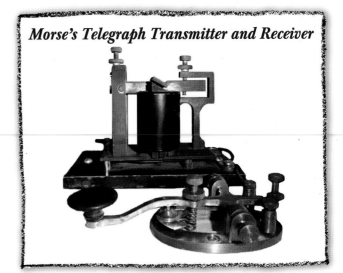

Morse's Telegraph Transmitter and Receiver

The Telegraph

In 1837, ten years before Alexander Graham Bell was born, Samuel F. B. Morse invented the electric telegraph. Using short and long pulses of energy, it could send a message in code over a wire. A telegraph operator translated the code into words.

There had to be a better way for people to communicate over long distances. Aleck was determined to find it. But he would need assistance. At a local machine shop, he met a talented electrician and mechanic: Thomas Watson. Thomas was the perfect person to help him with his experiments.

Together Aleck and Thomas began designing a device
that could transmit more than one message at a time,
each with a different vibration pattern, or pitch.
Oh, sure, there were failures—lots of them! But a
childhood spent experimenting with his brothers
had taught Aleck that the only real failure is to quit.
He and Thomas kept at it.

Months passed until one day Thomas adjusted a spring on a jammed transmitter. From the other room, Aleck's keen ears heard a faint *twang* through the receiver of their multiple telegraph invention. That little sound roared to Aleck's curiosity. Instead of transmitting the *beep-beeps* of dots and dashes, could he transmit the sound of a voice? Could he design a speaking telegraph?

TWAAAAANNNNG

Aleck's Transmitter Idea

Sound waves vibrate thin metal sheet.

Coil turns vibrations into electric signals.

Electric signals travel along wires.

Coil turns electric signals into magnetic field.

Receiver

Magnetic field vibrates thin metal sheet.

Nine months later, Aleck finally had a patent protecting his idea. Now all he needed was a working model to prove it.

Day after day each model they tested failed. Finally Thomas set up a receiver in one room. Aleck rigged a liquid transmitter in a separate room. They closed the doors. Aleck spoke into the cone. "Mr. Watson, come here. I want you!"

The "Gallows" Telephone (1875) was the first of Aleck's instruments to transform the sounds of speech into electrical current, but it was not loud enough. A year later he and Thomas invented the better model.

Thomas burst into the hall. "Mr. Bell, I heard you. I heard every word!"

The speaking telegraph worked! His voice had traveled from the transmitter, along a wire, and to a receiver at the other end.

Through the rest of the night, Aleck and Thomas fiddled with the device until they got it just right. Aleck danced a wild jig in celebration. The telephone was born!

How the Telephone Works

The telephone acts like an electric mouth. It sends electric current through an electromagnet and causes the receiver's membrane to vibrate, much like the membrane of a human ear. The vibrations hit the listener's eardrum, making it vibrate, too. The listener's eardrum hears these vibrations as the sounds spoken by the person at the other end.

From the beginning, the world all around spoke to Alexander Graham Bell. And he answered the call.

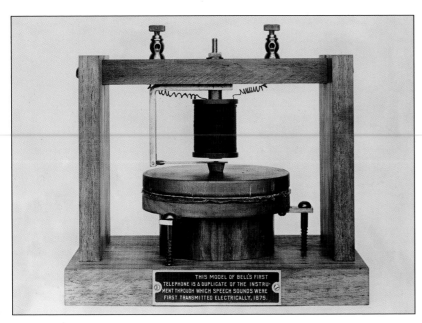

Bell's first telephone, 1876

The June Bug, July 4, 1908

ALECK'S INVENTIONS

Although Alexander Graham Bell was known as "the Father of the Telephone," during his life he won thirty-one patents–otherwise known as rights to one's inventions. Other ideas that never found their way out of his laboratory filled his notebooks, including designs for switchboards, phonographs, and an underwater distress signal. When an assassin shot President Garfield, Aleck invented a metal detector to locate the bullet. It would have worked if the doctors had not put the president on a mattress with metal springs. After his newborn son died, Aleck made a vacuum jacket to help premature babies breathe. He even developed an apparatus to remove the salt from seawater for thirsty shipwrecked sailors.

As the years passed, Aleck's ideas grew bigger–and loftier. Like the Wright brothers, he dreamed of manned flight. He built colossal kites using four-sided constructions called *tetrahedrons* that could lift a person into the air. But it was his flying machine, the June Bug, that proved to the world that controlled human flight was possible, when it soared more than one kilometer in 1908.

In the early 1900s, Aleck also built the fastest boat in the world at the time–the hydroplane, or "hydrodrome," as he called it. It rode on fins that lifted it up out of the water and achieved speeds of over seventy miles per hour. He even explored alternative fuels and described how smog could lead to the "greenhouse effect," or what today we call global warming.

Clearly Aleck was always listening to his curiosity and acting upon it. Many of his inventions continue to influence our lives today.

Aleck's Life

1847 — March 3; Alexander Bell is born in Edinburgh, Scotland

1863 — First teaching job in Elgin, Scotland

1867 — Brother Ted dies of tuberculosis

1868 — Begins teaching at a school for the Deaf in London

1870 — Brother Melly dies of tuberculosis. The Bells move to Canada, and Aleck becomes a Canadian citizen.

1871 — Moves to Boston, MA, to teach Deaf students

1872 — Opens his own oral-training school for teachers of the Deaf

1872 — Becomes a United States citizen

1874 — Meets Thomas A. Watson in a Boston machine shop

1875 — Thomas Watson becomes Aleck's assistant

1876 — March 10; First words heard through Aleck's telephone

1876 — June 25; Demonstrates the telephone at the Centennial Exhibition in Philadelphia

1877 — July 9; Forms the Bell Telephone Company with Gardiner Hubbard, Thomas Sanders, and Thomas Watson

1877 — July 11; Marries Mabel Hubbard

1881 — Invents a metal detector that can locate a bullet, following the shooting of President Garfield

1886 — Creates the Volta Bureau, a study center that researched causes of deafness and developed acoustic technologies

1887 — Meets Helen Keller

1890 — Invents a flat record and stylus needle

1891 — Begins flight experiments in Baddeck, Nova Scotia

1898 — Becomes the president of the National Geographic Society

1907 — Forms the Aerial Experiment Association to experiment with manned flight

1908 — Builds June Bug flying machine

1911 — Builds the first hydrofoil boat

1915 — January 25; Makes the first transcontinental telephone call

1922 — August 2; Alexander Graham Bell dies at his home, Beinn Bhreagh, in Baddeck, Nova Scotia, Canada

Alexander Graham Bell, 1877

A Note from the Author

Writers and artists share many characteristics with inventors. They are creative thinkers, naturally inquisitive, and help others see the world from a unique perspective. Perhaps, as a writer and artist, that is what first drew me to Aleck's story—the story of an inventor. During a visit to the Alexander Graham Bell Historic Site in Baddeck, Nova Scotia, I realized that, yes, Aleck was a brilliant inventor as an adult. But what impressed me most was his abundant curiosity and desire to help others, even as a child. This book is a celebration of that boy—the one who dared to ask questions and went in search of his own answers. It is a celebration of seeing the world through creative thinking.

My illustration technique also reflects Aleck's own interests. From a very young age, he was fascinated by photography, which was in its infancy at the time. I wanted my art for this book to reflect this interest. I've used new and old photographs—some my own and some from organizations that preserve and share artifacts from Aleck's life. These photographs and additional ephemera, collaged with my own original drawings, are meant to share a sense of the time period in which Aleck blossomed.

Photo Credits

UNITED STATES POSTAGE

ALEXANDER GRAHAM BELL

10¢

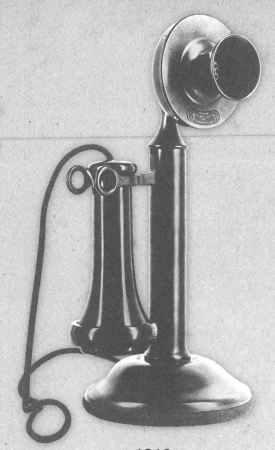

1910
Western Electric Candlestick
Desk Stand

1915
WE Model 20 Desk Stand

1913
Western Electric Wall Set